# HISTORIC DENVER GUIDES

# Historic Sacred Places of Denver

## MICHELLE PEARSON

PHOTOGRAPHY BY
ANNETTE VANASSE

HISTORIC DENVER, INC.

To all those working to preserve Historic Sacred Places in Denver, and to Connor, Alexander, Andrew, Raphael, Jeanetta, and Gregory, may you love history and architecture as much as your moms do.

This project was partially funded by a State Historical Fund grant award from the Colorado Historical Society and with the assistance of Historic Denver, Inc., Jeppesen, Ivan P. Morel & Associates, JVA Consulting with the U.S. Department of Health and Human Services Compassion Capital Fund, and the Scientific & Cultural Facilities District.

Scientific & Cultural Facilities District

International Standard Book Number: 0-914248-52-9
Text and photographs © 2004 Historic Denver, Inc.

Cover photo: Sacred Heart Church,
photograph © 2004 Historic Denver, Inc.

All rights reserved. No portion of this book, either photographs or text, may be used or reproduced in any form without the written permission of the publisher except in the case of brief quotations embodied in critical articles and reviews.

Individual or contributing structures in historic districts are marked **N⊞R** for National Register of Historic Places; **S⊞R** for Colorado State Register of Historic Properties; and **D⊞L** for Denver Landmarks. All **N⊞R** properties are also listed on the State Register.

Published by Historic Denver, Inc.
1536 Wynkoop Street, Suite 400A
Denver, Colorado 80202-1182

Printed by Mido Printing Company, Inc.
Editor: Marlene Blessing
Design and Composition: Cathy Calder, Blonde Ambition

# Contents

Acknowledgments....................................................4
Introduction.........................................................6
The Tours
   Tour One: Northeast Denver.....................................8
   Tour Two: Northwest Denver...................................26
   Tour Three: East/ Southeast Denver............................40
   Tour Four: Southwest Denver..................................58
   Tour Five: Central Denver.....................................74
Sources............................................................92
Sacred Places Index................................................93
Biographical Index.................................................94

THE GEOMETRIC DESIGN OF THIS CEILING DOME IN THE ZEN CENTER (PAGE 30)
ADDS BEAUTY AND LIGHT TO THE SANCTUARY.

# Acknowledgments

On behalf of Historic Denver, Inc., and the Sacred Landmarks Preservation Program, I would like to thank the Colorado Historical Society State Historical Fund and JVA Consulting, through the Colorado Compassion Initiative, for supporting the publication of this book. Programs such as this ensure that preservation education continues in Colorado.

This book would not have been possible without the dedication, patience, and research assistance of Nicole Hernandez of the Sacred Places Preservation Program at Historic Denver, Inc. She is to be commended for her work to protect and preserve sacred places in Denver and for the pivotal role she played in the creation of this guide. Additionally, my sincere thanks are extended to Kathleen Brooker of Historic Denver for supporting the addition of this unique guide to the quality collection of Denver guides Historic Denver has previously published.

The artistic eye of Annette Vanasse is reflected in the wonderful photos that accompany the text of this book. Her hard work and attention to detail have made a difference in the way these sacred sites are presented to the reader.

Many thanks to the volunteers and staff of the various sacred places in this guide for their assistance with the reviews of historical information. Thanks to the staff at the Colorado History Society library, the Office of Archaeology and Historic Preservation, and the Colorado Historical Society for their assistance with the research for this guide. Meg Van Ness has been especially helpful with her assistance with the COMPASS system.

The members of the Sacred Landmarks Steering Committee and the staff of Historic Denver, Inc., have been invaluable for their support of this endeavor and their selection and review of locations to be included in this publication.

Sharon Burke, Tom Crane, Janis Day, Fr. Gene Emrisek, Lilianne Fischer, Lina Howe, Robert Howe, Tim Howe, Dina Johnson, Judith Pearson, Don Reeves, John Riley, Marie Shaw, Fr. John Toepfer, Vicki Murphy, and Sue Myers have been extremely helpful with a variety of tasks associated with the completion of this project.

Many thanks are extended to Cathy Calder and Marlene Blessing for their hard work in preparing this guide for publication and for their insight and thoughtful suggestions. They have made a difference in both how this guide looks and reads.

Finally, I would like to thank my husband, Kirk. You have endured your wife's passion for history and books and selflessly gave of yourself in countless ways to make this book happen. Thank you for bringing me home to Denver.

A SIMPLE CROSS TOPS THE METAL DOME OF THE MISSION-STYLE
ST. PATRICK'S CHURCH (PAGE 36) IN WEST DENVER.

VARIOUS ELEMENTS, INCLUDING THE ROSE WINDOW, ADD DECORATIVE ELEMENTS TO THIS GOTHIC REVIVAL CATHEDRAL OF THE IMMACULATE CONCEPTION. (PAGE 88)

## INTRODUCTION

This guide was developed under the vision of the Sacred Landmarks Preservation Program, a division of Historic Denver, Inc. The Sacred Landmarks Preservation Program joined forces with Historic Denver, Inc., in the fall of 2000. As a secular program, it strives to ensure that historic sacred places will remain centers for community life and programs long into the future.

Recognizing the special nature and the value of historic sacred places in the state of Colorado and in the city of Denver to the communities in which they serve, the Sacred Landmarks Preservation Program seeks to share these sites with the wider community of citizens who are interested in the art and architecture that these historic churches harbor. Many of the historic sacred places in Denver are hidden historic gems, as well as vital community centers.

In 2003, the National Trust for Historic Preservation listed urban sacred places as one of the eleven most endangered places in America. Along with other national historic sites, historic sacred places are struggling to survive in a time of limited capital budgets, soaring real estate values, and changing demographics. This struggle is a day-to-day reality for many of the historic sacred places in the heart of Denver that people have grown to know and love.

Sacred places play important roles in the communities in which they are located. Research has shown that sacred places serve as de facto community and service centers, providing critical programming for the poor and for those looking for a sense of belonging in their community. Historic sacred places, many of which are located in inner-city communities throughout the country, give hope to those in need by offering a critical link between those who live in the city and the services they need to survive on a daily basis. Research documents that without these historic buildings and their congregants, approximately 76 percent of programs that serve the community would not exist at all.

Historic sacred places are at risk. Threatened by years of deferred maintenance and financial disinvestments, sacred places are now faced with the challenge of sustaining both their buildings and programming through new fundraising efforts and preservation programming. This is often a daunting task, but one that has been greatly supported by the Colorado Historic Society's State Historic Fund, the Sacred Landmarks Preservation Program, Historic Denver, Inc. and many other outstanding organizations within the city of Denver. Most importantly, preservation efforts have come from the hearts of the congregations and communities that these churches serve. The people of Denver are working to preserve the sacred places that they cherish, and in doing so they are ensuring a historical legacy for future generations.

The historic buildings outlined in this guide are but a sampling of the many historic sacred places that help to create the vibrant cultural tapestry of the city of Denver.

# TOUR ONE: NORTHEAST DENVER

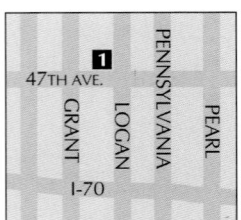
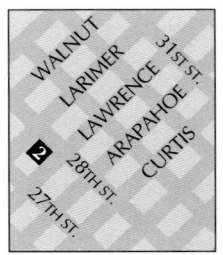
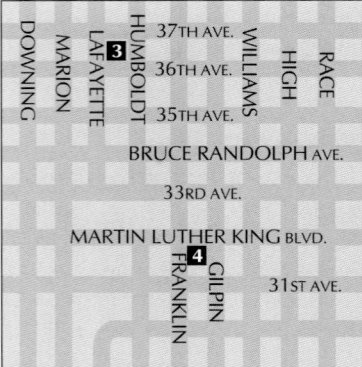

▲ North

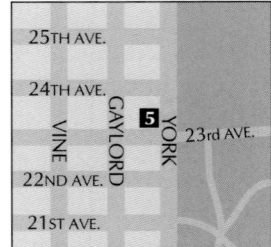
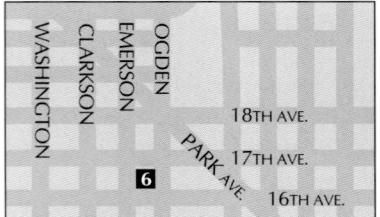

# KEY

1. 349 East 47th Avenue
   (Holy Transfiguration of Christ Cathedral)
2. 2760 Larimer Street
   (Sacred Heart Catholic Church)
3. 3601 Humboldt Street
   (Annunciation Catholic Church)
4. 1631 Martin Luther King Jr. Boulevard
   (Denver Gospel Church)
5. 2305 Gaylord Street
   (St. Ignatius Loyola)
6. 1601 Ogden Street
   (St. Paul's United Methodist Church)
7. 933 East 24th Avenue
   (Zion Baptist Church)

# HOLY TRANSFIGURATION OF CHRIST CATHEDRAL
349 EAST 47TH AVENUE

Architectural Style: GOTHIC REVIVAL
Built: 1898–1904  Cost: UNKNOWN  Architect: UNKNOWN

Built as a small church to serve the community in which it was placed, the Church of the Holy Transfiguration continues its tradition of welcoming new immigrants, today serving newcomers from such faraway places as Eritrea.

Built to meet the needs of the earliest business enclaves in the city, construction of the church was begun and completed in 1898. It was consecrated in 1904 by Bishop Tikhon of San Francisco, who later became the Patriarch of Moscow and a saint of the Russian Orthodox Church. The congregation is composed of Carpatho-Russians, Serbs, and Moldavians who used to work in the smelters, slaughterhouses, and brickyards of Denver. This group founded the church and has maintained it for decades.

In 1972, the neighborhood was changing and the church was strong and healthy and ready to move. At the last moment, the church council president Nickolai Zeniuk refused to abandon the church and the pastoral council agreed. This caused uproar between those who wanted to move and those who wanted to stay. The parish lost about half of its membership. Later in the 1970s, the city of Denver proposed to industrialize the Globeville area completely. Residents derailed the plan, and the church has since gone through a renaissance.

The exterior of the church is built in a Gothic Revival style with a semicircular wall on one side to represent the rounded apse of wooden churches seen in Eastern Europe. The church is composed of brick, which was covered with stucco in the 1920s.

The interior of the church is a haven for icons, murals, and artwork representative of the Eastern Orthodox tradition. Historical artwork from the early beginnings of the church is intertwined with new commissioned icons from American iconographers and various Eastern European artists.

(TOP) ICONS, ARTWORK, STAINED GLASS, MURALS, AND STATUARY FILL THE EXQUISITE INTERIOR OF THE CHURCH. (BOTTOM) IN THE REAR OF THE SANCTUARY, A DETAILED ICON SITS BETWEEN DELICATE STAINED-GLASS WINDOWS.

## SACRED HEART CATHOLIC CHURCH D&L
### 2760 LARIMER STREET

Architectural Style: GOTHIC REVIVAL
Built: 1879   Cost: LAND, $1,500; BUILDING, UNKNOWN
Architect: EMMETT ANTHONY

Hailed as the oldest continually operating church in Denver, this parish has served the community of Denver for over one hundred years. Painstaking restoration and preservation efforts over the last five years have brought the building out of severe disrepair, and the landmark church now serves this predominately Hispanic community.

Originally built for an upper-class Irish and Italian community in 1879, the Sacred Heart Church was established in a neighborhood that was growing because of the arrival of the railroads in 1870. The church had many prominent citizens as members, including Horace and Elizabeth "Baby Doe" Tabor and Julia Greeley. After Horace Tabor's funeral at Sacred Heart, Baby Doe left Denver to return to the mountains and their famous "Matchless Mine."

In 1892, the congregation began the Sacred Heart Aid Society to serve the poor. Later, in 1925, the Little Flower Social Center began operation to offer food, clothing, and shelter to all who asked. Today the mission continues as Sacred Heart supports the community in many of the same ways. Over time, the demographics of the neighborhood have changed. Sacred Heart's parishioners are now primarily working-class Hispanic-Americans.

The exterior of the church is a mix of architectural styles, but is primarily Gothic. The church has a restored wooden staircase entrance, rebuilt to historic specifications. Simple stained-glass windows accent the brick exterior of the building.

The interior of the church is laid out in a Latin cross format, with exposed wood beams and a magnificent wooden altar. Murals with Hispanic influence have been painted on the ceiling to add a cultural perspective to the church, and Our Lady of Guadalupe, the patron saint of Mexico, is evident in the building through the use of murals, statuary, and icons that reflect her image.

(TOP) THE TALL RESTORED STEEPLE CAPS THE OLDEST CHURCH IN DENVER. (TOP RIGHT) EXPOSED WOOD BEAMS IN THE CHURCH'S INTERIOR HAVE BEEN RESTORED BY HAND AND DECORATIVELY PAINTED.

## 3. ANNUNCIATION CATHOLIC CHURCH
### 3601 HUMBOLDT STREET

NR DL

Architectural Style: GOTHIC REVIVAL
Built: 1904  Cost: UNKNOWN  Architect: UNKNOWN

Annunciation Catholic Church is one of the most highly visible, beautifully crafted, and culturally significant buildings in the Cole neighborhood of Denver. Listed at the federal, state and local levels, the church is one of only three individually designated sites in the Cole neighborhood.

Since 1883, Annunciation has played a role in the history of Denver. It was established to serve the Irish, Slavic, and German immigrants who worked in the smelters and for the railroads in northeast Denver. Its 1904 construction, under the direction of Fr. Henry Robinson, helped to stall the encroachment of industrial development from the South Platte River bottoms, thus preserving the immediate neighborhoods and protecting the neighborhoods east and south of it.

Today Annunciation continues to be a refuge for the newest immigrants to Denver. Under the direction of the Capuchin Franciscans of Mid-America, and with the assistance of the Sisters of Charity of Leavenworth, who run Annunciation School, the church provides spiritual, social, and educational support as well as critical emergency and health services to the community, regardless of religious affiliation.

Considered by many to be a "hidden jewel box," Annunciation is a recognizable landmark in the neighborhood. Crafted in the Gothic style, it is simple in design with contrasting red brick and sandstone exterior elements. The square tower from the original plans was left unfinished and does not have a steeple.

In contrast, the flamboyant Romanesque interior houses a myriad of artwork, including oil paintings, frescoes, scagliola (imitation marble), statuary, and a Carrara marble altar. The church holds a magnificent collection of stained-glass windows from Germany, created by Franz Meyer and F. X. Zettler, that are considered to be some of the best in the United States.

(TOP) THE ROMANESQUE-STYLE INTERIOR OF ANNUNCIATION IS FILLED WITH EXCELLENT EXAMPLES OF SCULPTURE, STAINED GLASS, SCAGLIOLA, AND ARTWORK.
(LEFT) THE DETAILING ON THE CARRARA MARBLE ALTAR EXEMPLIFIES THE OUTSTANDING CRAFTSMANSHIP EVIDENT IN THE INTERIOR.

## 4. DENVER GOSPEL CHURCH  S&R
### 1631 EAST MARTIN LUTHER KING JR. BOULEVARD

Architectural Style: GOTHIC REVIVAL
Built: 1910  Cost: $16,000  Architect: UNKNOWN

Known originally as Bethany Swedish Evangelical Church, Denver Gospel Church is an excellent architectural example of the Gothic Revival church. Built in 1910, the church, under the direction of Rev. Dr. Robert Ascell, originally served a small enclave of Swedish immigrants who lived in the Cole and Whittier neighborhoods. When the site was purchased, the congregation began raising funds to complete the building. The basement was completed first and the first service was held on Easter morning in 1910. In 1923, the sanctuary was completed and the congregation met in the upper building for the first time.

Through the history of Denver, this area has been affected by racism, segregation, and integration. These movements and the succession of changes they brought affected the congregation as well. In March of 1957 the building was sold to the Denver Gospel Church, which was comprised of predominantly African-American families.

Since this time, the church has remained a strong neighborhood institution, serving those in need. Community programs such as a youth club, prison ministry, and clothing and food bank have served the residents of the Cole and Whittier neighborhoods and still do today.

Denver Gospel Church embodies characteristics of the late Gothic Revival style. The brick and sandstone on its exterior are still intact, and the building retains much of its original integrity. In contrast to larger Gothic churches, it has a smaller square steeple and blends in with the neighborhood. The interior of the church also preserves much of the original character of the building and contains an outstanding collection of stained glass. The windows are the major focus of the sanctuary, adding both light and beauty to the structure.

A decorative metal pinnacle caps the gable in the front of the church.

Decorative brickwork and sandstone frame the double-arched doorway.

## 5  ST. IGNATIUS LOYOLA CHURCH  N☒R
### 2305 GAYLORD STREET

Architectural Style: GOTHIC REVIVAL
Built: 1923–4  Cost: $224,000
Architects: FRANK W. FREWEN JR., FRANK E. MOUNTJOY

In 1921, Fr. Charles McDonnell, fourth pastor of Loyola Chapel in Denver, envisioned a large church built to hold his burgeoning congregation. Father McDonnell's vision was realized with the dedication of the church on October 12, 1924 at its new site at 23rd and York. More than 3,000 people attended the ceremonies, said to be among the finest in the history of Denver.

On May 21, 1935, the name was officially changed to the Roman Catholic Congregation of Sacred Heart–Loyola, and the church was administered by the pastor of Sacred Heart Church. In 1944, the site became an independent church with its own pastor and is currently the only Jesuit-administered church in Denver.

The neighborhood around Loyola originally comprised German, Irish, and Italian families and was predominately middle- and upper-class residential. A large portion of the residents worked in the central business district of Denver. Over time, the demographics changed and today Loyola hosts a large component of African-American members, with some Hispanic and Anglo members in attendance as well.

In the words of one parishioner, "The church is the history of an urban neighborhood. From a wealthy temple, to a poor church in need of restoration, St. Ignatius Loyola has always reflected the people and trends of the Whittier neighborhood."

Hailed as one of two churches designed by architect Frank W. Frewen Jr., and his only Gothic Tudor work, the church's exterior has a strong vertical emphasis.

Loyola's interior features a Carrara marble altar, oak paneling, sixteen massive painted stained-glass windows, and a painting by Austrian painter Anton Schwaezler. A Celotex ceiling, known for its acoustic properties, allows any uttered word to be heard from any corner of the church.

(TOP) THE GOTHIC TRACERY AND TOWER EXEMPLIFY THE STYLE OF THIS CHURCH.
(LEFT) ITS UNIQUE BAPTISMAL FONT IS A HIGHLIGHT OF THE INTERIOR OF THE CHURCH.

## 6. ST. PAUL'S UNITED METHODIST CHURCH
### 1601 OGDEN STREET

**NR DL**

Architectural Style: CLASSICAL REVIVAL
Built: 1910  Cost: UNKNOWN  Architect: B. HYDER

Located in the Swallow Hill Historic District **NR**, **DL**, St. Paul's United Methodist Church is a cornerstone of the community. Prominent as a landmark, it is one of the many buildings that provide unique character to this district.

Built in 1910 by a congregation in need of a larger facility, it served a diverse community of working- to upper-class residents. Started with donations from a handful of unnamed Denverites, the church's construction began when B. Hyder created his Classical Revival plans for it. These plans mimicked the designs of many of the buildings being constructed in Denver during this period.

The arched windows and decorative columns with ionic capitals on the exterior of the building reflect a Classical Revival style. Detailed brickwork highlights the exterior in beige rather than the standard red. Egg-and-dart details and dentil molding are evident on all facades of the structure. Arched stained-glass windows add visual texture to the front and side facades.

The interior of the church has decorative wood molding and excellent examples of stained glass.

(TOP) ST. PAUL'S STANDS AS A LANDMARK IN THIS HISTORIC NEIGHBORHOOD. (BOTTOM) CLASSICAL ARCHITECTURAL DETAILS SUCH AS EGG-AND-DART AND DENTIL MOLDING GRACE THE EXTERIOR.

## 7. ZION BAPTIST CHURCH
### 933 EAST 24TH AVENUE

**NR DL**

Architectural Style: ROMANESQUE REVIVAL
Built: 1892  Cost: UNKNOWN
Architect: : FRANK H. JACKSON AND GEORGE F. RIVINIUS

Zion Baptist Congregation is considered one of the oldest African-American congregations in the United States, and the oldest west of the Mississippi. Since its inception, the church has played a prominent role as a leader in Denver society and as a community institution that serves those in need.

The original members of the church built it in 1892 under the name of Calvary Baptist Church. The site was selected partially because the ethnic diversity of the neighborhoods in Denver had changed, and partially because by moving to this site the church was more accessible to its membership. Church leaders of Calvary Baptist Church acknowledge this in their historical records. Walter McDuffie Potter and Ira Clark were circuit riders who temporarily ministered to the congregation until William Norrid, a freed slave who once led a rebellion, became the first pastor.

Norrid was one of the church's most notable leaders. He served as a delegate to the city of Denver and the state Republican convention, and signed a petition asking the United States Congress to halt the statehood process for Colorado until Colorado offered equal opportunity for "colored people." Buried in 1904 in Riverside Cemetery, Norrid is remembered for starting the first colored Masonic group in the United States, which later turned into the Rocky Mountain Lodge of the Elks. Today his gravestone remains unmarked.

Besides Norrid, many other prominent Coloradans have called Zion Baptist home. For many years, the prominent members of Denver's Black social community were members of Zion because of the accomplishments of several pastors in the church's history. These included Rev. John E. Ford and his wife Justina Warren Ford, the first "Black Baby Doctor," and Rev. Wendell Theodore Liggins, the latter of whom served the church for more than fifty years.

(TOP) DETAILED STAINED GLASS
IS A HIGHLIGHT IN ALL SECTIONS
OF THIS CHURCH.
(BOTTOM) THE SQUARE STONE TOWER
DECORATED BY DENTIL MOLDING IS A
NEIGHBORHOOD LANDMARK.

Even after several churches were created from Zion, including Central Baptist and Union Baptist, Zion was still the leader of the social community. Civil War veteran Rufus K. Felton was the first African-American teacher in the Colorado Territory and one of Zion's first members. Many famous people are on record as having spoken at Zion, including James Weldon Johnson, author of the Negro National Anthem "Lift Every Voice and Sing"; A. Phillip Randolph, a civil rights activist; Walter Storey, the first president of the NAACP; Richard Lamm; Pat Schroeder; and Rev. Jesse Jackson. Current members include former Denver Mayor Wellington E. Webb and former Colorado State Representative Wilma G. Webb.

Zion continues to remain active in the community. With over 900 people on the church roster, and 300 members attending regularly, the church offers many programs for its members and for the neighboring community. As part of its mission, Zion supports community outreach programming that includes employment assistance, prayer ministries, and emergency services programming that benefits those in need.

The exterior of the Zion Baptist Church has been restored to its original Gothic style with a few architectural and cultural additions, such as the neon Zion sign on the corner of the building. The church's square stone tower and decorative dentil molding highlight its exterior and provide the neighborhood with a distinctive visual landmark.

The interior is decorated with historic lighting, restored wood and metal railings, and a large collection of religious and decorative stained glass.

The sanctuary features an arched entrance.

# TOUR TWO: NORTHWEST DENVER

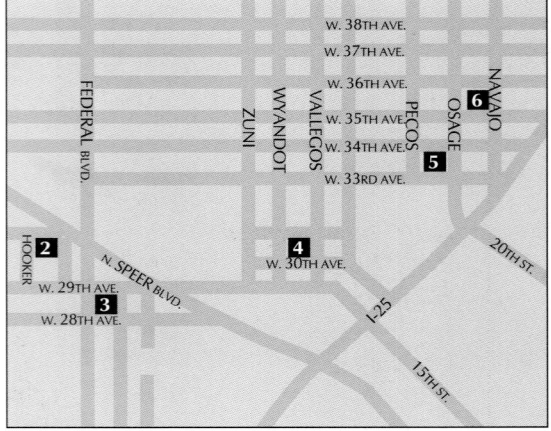

# KEY

1. 2222 West 32nd Avenue
   (Chapel of Our Merciful Savior)
2. 3101 West 31st Avenue
   (Zen Center of Denver)
3. 3005 West 29th Avenue
   (St. Dominic's Church)
4. 2215 West 30th Avenue
   (Asbury Methodist Episcopal Church)
5. 3325 Pecos Street
   (St. Patrick's Church)
6. 3549 Navajo Street
   (Our Lady of Mount Carmel Church)

# CHAPEL OF OUR MERCIFUL SAVIOR
## 2222 WEST 32ND AVENUE

NR DL

Architectural Style: GOTHIC REVIVAL
Built: 1890  Cost: UNKNOWN  Architect: JAMES MURDOCH

Built originally as All Saints Episcopal Church in 1890, Our Chapel of Our Merciful Savior is an excellent example of a small church built to serve the needs of lower middle–class working families. Today the church serves that same constituency and remains virtually unaltered or changed from the day that it was constructed.

The parish originated in 1874, when it was organized as a mission. On December 4, 1889, the parish was formally organized, and in 1890 land was purchased for the present site. James Murdoch was chosen as architect. Construction was completed in September of 1890.

In the late 1890s, the parish was primarily composed of Germans working in the breweries along the Platte River. In 1893, a large contingent of Welsh and Cornish families became members when many Colorado silver mines were closed and they were forced to relocate to Denver to secure work. Few of these members were wealthy, but all were proud, independent, and supportive of the parish. Due to a lack of funds, the church was never altered or modernized. In 1961, a new church was built at 37th and Yates and the old structure was renamed to its current name of Chapel of Our Merciful Savior. Today the parish still provides a variety of outreach services to the poor.

The building is rectangular with a square tower and steeple on the northwest corner of the front facade. Gothic arched windows decorate the exterior and the west facade. A rose window dominates the front gable.

The interior of the church retains the original pews, floors, and walls. Hammered beams and a wainscoted ceiling in a herringbone pattern accentuate the rose window. The original 1890 Farrand and Votey organ was recently restored and is fully functional.

(LEFT) THE SMALL ANGEL STATUE IS IN THE IMAGE OF A DAUGHTER OF ONE OF THE FIRST PASTORS. (BOTTOM) THE ROSE WINDOW, WITH ITS ORGANIC DESIGN, ILLUMINATES THE SANCTUARY BELOW.

## ZEN CENTER OF DENVER
### 3101 WEST 31ST AVENUE

NR

Architectural Style: CLASSICAL REVIVAL
Built: 1920  Cost: UNKNOWN
Architects: BURNHAM F. HOYT, MERRILL H. HOYT

Introduced by Rev. Mary Baker Eddy in the 1870s, Christian Science theology and practice came to Denver in 1885. In 1891, this congregation incorporated as the Fourth Church of Christ, Scientist and hired the architectural firm of Hoyt and Hoyt to design their new place of worship. As with many other Christian Science buildings, the design is Classical Revival and reflects the teachings and beliefs held by the sect, including visual calm and harmony of spirit.

The church building is representative of the "City Beautiful" movement promoted by Mayor Robert Speer in Denver after his election to office until his death in 1918. As Speer built public buildings in the Classic Revival style, private churches and residents were likewise inspired to erect elegant buildings that shaped the neighborhoods of Denver. Hoyt and Hoyt followed this example and were responsible for the design of other prominent buildings in Denver, including the Denver Press Club and the Park Hill Library.

In 1998 the Zen Center purchased the building to give itself room to grow and to provide a public venue for program offerings to the community, such as open meditation and introductory seminars on Zen Buddhism.

This three-story building is designed in a triangular-shaped plan, with a hipped roof of terra-cotta tiles. Decorative dentil molding complements the highly decorated eaves. Constructed of blond brick and sandstone, the building is characterized by large stone pediments that are supported by columns with Corinthian capitals.

While renovation has taken place to transform the space from one religion to another, the community has worked to preserve the historical integrity of the building. The interior of the church features arched decorative ceilings, decorative plaster elements, terrazzo floors, and the original skylight and historic lighting.

Restoration of the interior has been carefully done to enhance the reuse of space for those practicing the Buddhist religion.

The building's Classical Revival exterior reflects the theology of its original inhabitants.

# ST. DOMINIC'S CHURCH
## 3005 WEST 29TH AVENUE

Architectural Style: LATE GOTHIC REVIVAL
Built: 1921–6  Cost: $270,000  Architect: ROBERT WILLISON

Designed by Robert Willison, St. Dominic's Church is considered a tribute to the "hopes and aspirations of Denver's Dominican religious community." Fr. J. T. Murphy and Bishop Nicholas Matz created the parish on October 6, 1889. The parish was run by the Dominicans and had an established convent of Dominican sisters to teach at the school. Originally located at 25th and Decatur Streets, the parish was composed primarily of Irish, German, and Italian constituents, who worked for the railroad, mining, and agriculture industries.

In 1915, a fund was established to build a larger church. Although an influenza epidemic and World War I affected many in the congregation, the parish still continued to raise funds. Construction began in 1921. After the church's dedication in 1926, the parish redoubled its effort to build a strong Catholic community in response to the increase of Ku Klux Klan activity in Denver. A parish credit union was established in 1933, and a retreat center in Nederland was built in the 1930s. A new school was erected on the site in 1951, and subsequently closed in 1973. Today, the parish serves a diverse community comprising Anglo, Asian, African-American, and Hispanic members.

The exterior of the church has a symmetrical facade with a strong vertical element. The front facade includes a double recessed portal entry, highlighted by a large rose window. The church is designed as a two-story structure in the Latin cross plan with north-south transepts and a front narthex.

The interior of the church displays architectural elements, including groined vaulting, perpendicular Gothic arches, and paneled buttresses. The church artwork includes Gothic windows, historic Gothic Revival lighting, and a crucifix created in honor of those serving in World War II carved by artist Fr. Tom McGlynn.

Vaulted ceilings and other Gothic features help make the interior visually stunning.

Detailed stonework on the interior of the building.

# ASBURY METHODIST EPISCOPAL CHURCH
## 2215 WEST 30TH AVENUE

Architectural Style: RICHARDSONIAN ROMANESQUE
Built: 1890–3   Cost: $75,000
Architects: FRANK KIDDER AND JOHN HUMPHREYS

As Denver's population swelled in the latter part of the nineteenth century, churches were quickly erected to serve the needs of growing communities. Built in the growing community known as Highland, Asbury Methodist Episcopal was an example of one such church.

Originally serving a community of Welsh and Cornish immigrants, the church was erected in 1890–3, coinciding with an influx of immigrants who left Colorado's mining towns after the devaluation of silver. The congregation, many of whom were working class, raised the money for the church through donations, known as subscriptions, and pew fees charged to members. Today, the church is privately owned but rented to the Calvary Greenwood congregation.

The name Asbury is common among churches of the Methodist sect. Derived from Francis Asbury, a Methodist preacher from Britain who was consecrated as General Superintendent of American Methodism by John Wesley in 1784, the name is used throughout the world. Asbury is responsible for the large growth of the Methodist population in this country through his work as a traveling minister and leader in the church.

Architects Kidder and Humphreys were hired to construct the building with a large, landmark bell tower that is still visible today from the downtown Sixteenth Street Mall. Constructed of red brick and sandstone from Manitou Springs and rhyolite, the church is designed in a Richardsonian Romanesque style. Beautiful exterior doors are mounted on the front facade of the church.

A collection of stained glass and the sanctuary ceiling formed in the shape of a Greek cross are highlights of the church's interior. The organ, constructed by Charles Anderson in 1876, is the oldest working pipe organ in continuous use in Colorado.

ON THE EXTERIOR OF THE CHURCH, THE DETAIL IN THE STONE CARVINGS REFLECTS THE FINE CRAFTSMANSHIP.

TWO-TONED STONEWORK HIGHLIGHTS THIS FULL EXTERIOR VIEW OF ASBURY.

# ST. PATRICK'S CHURCH
## 3325 PECOS STREET

**NR DL**

Architectural Style: MISSION REVIVAL
Built: 1907–10  Cost: UNKNOWN
Architects: F. C. WAGNER AND HARRY JAMES MANNING

Located on a bluff overlooking the city of Denver and the Platte River, this mission-style church was once a dominant feature of the Denver skyline. The church is distinctive in its features as it is one of the few mission-style churches to be built in Denver. Additionally, the original mission of the church, "to serve all people of the area, Catholic and non-Catholic alike," is still in place today.

Bishop Joseph Machebeuf established St. Patrick's parish in 1881 as the only Catholic church in west Denver. Eight other parishes now reside within its original boundaries. Fr. Joseph Carrigan studied early mission churches and shared his dream of a mission church with the parish. Land was purchased in 1906, and the Wagner and Manning architectural firm was hired to design the church.

At odds with Bishop Nicholas Matz, Carrigan and the parishioners quarreled with the bishop when work on the church was started without approval from the bishop's office. Later, Carrigan conveniently laid the cornerstone when the bishop was out of town, and was eventually removed from the parish. Before leaving, he realized the completion of the parish and his dream.

St. Patrick's is a cornerstone of the Irish and Hispanic communities of Denver. Today the church is home to the Capuchin order of the Poor Clares and their cloister and still serves the poor.

The church is a two-story rectangular building with a simple mission-style design. Towers at the front corners of the church are capped with metal domes and surround a porch and arched entry.

Inside the church are a collection of stained-glass windows created in the United States of foreign glass and a collection of Stations of the Cross, housed in elaborately carved Italian marble frames.

(TOP) WITH ARCHED DETAILS AND MULTIPLE TOWERS, THE EXTERIOR EAST FACADE REFLECTS THE MISSION STYLE OF THE CHURCH.
(BOTTOM) THE INTERIOR COURTYARD OF ST. PATRICK'S IS NOW A CLOISTER AND HOME TO THE CAPUCHIN POOR CLARES OF DENVER.

## 6 OUR LADY OF MOUNT CARMEL CHURCH
### 3549 NAVAJO STREET

D&L

Architectural Style: ROMANESQUE REVIVAL
Built: 1894, REBUILT 1898  Cost: UNKNOWN  Architect: FRANK DAMASCIO

With the arrival of Fr. Mariano Lepore, a champion of poor immigrants in Denver, the guidance of Mother Frances Cabrini, and the growth of the Italian neighborhoods in the west side of the city, the concept of the establishment of an Italian-centered church was born. Seemingly at once, Our Lady of Mount Carmel church became a reality rather than a dream.

Established to serve the large population of Italian immigrants in Denver, Mount Carmel was first dedicated in 1894 on Palm Sunday by Bishop Nicholas Matz. After a fire leveled the building in 1898, two different groups of Italian community members raced to complete new churches in its place. Bishop Matz supported the rebuilding of Mount Carmel rather than of the rival church, the Chapel of Saint Rocco: He refused to consecrate the latter or to send a pastor to the site. Rather, the new Our Lady of Mount Carmel was dedicated on December 18, 1904, with much Italian fanfare. Matz followed the suggestion of Mother Cabrini and asked the Servite Fathers to run the new church. Fr. Lepore was conspicuously absent at the dedication, having been mysteriously assassinated in 1903 by a local laborer.

As the Italian community grew and spread out into suburban parishes after World War II, the parish membership dropped. Today the church still serves a diverse community and holds onto its Italian heritage through traditions that have been in place from its humble beginning.

The exterior of the church shines over the rooftops of the neighborhood with copper-topped domes and white crosses. The church has detailed stone masonry work and a beautiful cross on the rear red brick chimney in the alley.

Inside, frescoes, statuary, and woodwork give the church an Italian feel. Rightly so, since the church was originally the "hub of Little Italy."

(TOP) DETAILS OF THE EXTERIOR STONE AND CAPITAL SHOW THE CRAFTSMANSHIP OF THE MASONS WHO BUILT MOUNT CARMEL.
(BOTTOM) TWIN TOWERS CAP

# TOUR THREE: EAST/SOUTHEAST DENVER

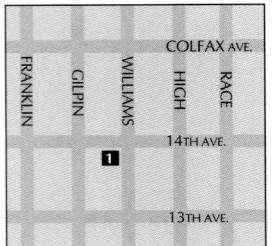
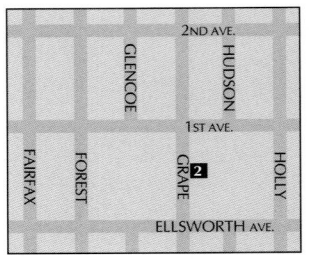

▲
North

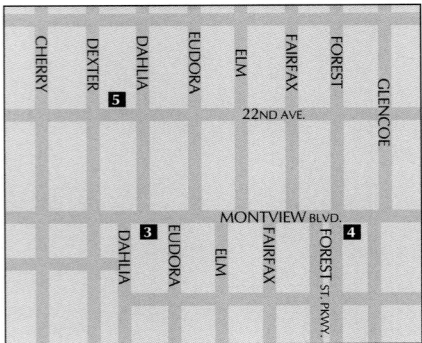
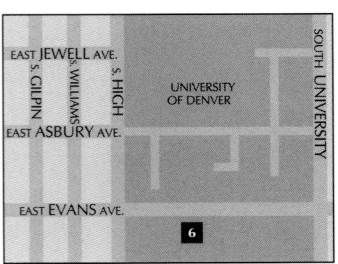

# KEY

1. 1400 Williams Street
   (First Divine Science Church of Denver)
2. 51 Grape Street
   (Temple Emanuel)
3. 1980 Dahlia Street
   (Montview Boulevard Presbyterian Church)
4. 5209 Montview Boulevard
   (Park Hill United Methodist Church)
5. 2201 Dexter Street
   (St. Thomas Episcopal Church)
6. 2199 South Vine Street
   (Evans Memorial Chapel, University of Denver Campus)

# FIRST DIVINE SCIENCE CHURCH OF DENVER
1400 WILLIAMS STREET

Architectural Style: CLASSICAL REVIVAL
Built: 1921–2   Architect: JULES JACQUES BENOIS BENEDICT

Designed by noted architect J. J. B. Benedict and home to Denver's first woman minister, the First Divine Science Church plays an important role in the history of Denver.

The Colorado College of Divine Science was established on October 26, 1898. Services were first held at the Plymouth Hotel at 16th and Broadway in 1899. One of the most famous ministers from this church, Nona L. Brooks, was ordained on December 1, 1898, and served as a minister at the church. Under Brooks, the congregation grew rapidly and a larger site was needed eventually. The site at 14th and Williams, comprising six lots, was purchased in 1921. Construction occurred in 1921, and the dedication took place in 1922.

Education has remained a primary focus of the congregation and the Brooks Divinity School, originally housed at this site, still exists today under the name Brooks Center for Spirituality. The majority of the ordained ministers of Divine Science in the United States, including well-known authors Emmet Fox and Joseph Murphy, received their theology certificates from Denver. In addition to its role in the Divine Science community, the church hosts lectures, concerts, and classes for the community.

This church is considered one of architect Benedict's later mature works and is both restrained and balanced in its design. The exterior of the church reflects the Classical Revival style, with columns flanking the entry colonnade and windows. A decorative roof and terra-cotta ornamentation accentuate the entry. This ornamentation is also seen around the windows and at the roofline.

The interior of the church has remained virtually untouched. Historical light fixtures remain, and the seating in the nave is square and surrounded by balconies with theaterlike seating. The interior is capped by a large skylight, which provides both light and decoration.

THE SYMMETRICAL VAULTED CEILING WITH SKYLIGHTS ADDS
DRAMA TO THE INTERIOR OF THE BUILDING.

DETAILED TERRA-COTTA ELEMENTS ON THIS CHURCH
ARE UNIQUE IN THIS WESTERN REGION.

## 2. TEMPLE EMANUEL
### 51 GRAPE STREET

N&R

Architectural Style: MODERN MOVEMENT
Built: 1953–60   Cost: $2,438,000   Architect: PERCIVAL GOODMAN

Located in the Hilltop section of Denver, Temple Emanuel is one of the largest Jewish congregations in the West. Beginning in 1939 and continuing after World War II, the large growth of the population of Jews in the United States placed pressures to expand on the congregations that served them. This was the case in Denver, and Temple Emanuel started to look for a new location, its fourth in the history of the city. Following the growth trends of the post–World War II era, the congregation was outgrowing its space and needed a larger, more convenient location for a temple. To achieve this, they moved toward the suburbs of Denver, away from their original inner-city location.

Due to segregated housing practices at the time, many of Denver's Jewish families began to move to outlying areas, primarily to Hilltop. Other Jewish facilities were located there, such as the Jewish Community Center and the Hillel Academy. Temple Emanuel followed suit. After purchasing two lots in the midst of Hilltop for $900,000, the congregation selected architect Percival Goodman through a competitive process. He created a modernistic building, a style being embraced during this period that embodied the ideal of the "future's triumphs being held over the travails of the past."

Influenced by the Usonian style, which is based on Frank Lloyd Wright's vision of naturalism, the temple is streamlined and marries form and function, which is a hallmark of this style. Additionally, it is designed under one of Percival Goodman's key tenets of synagogue design: "the form of the building is dictated by its tripartite function as a House of Prayer, a House of Study, and a House of Assembly." With this in mind, Goodman designed the main temple with areas for education, worship, and community.

Created of Colorado red Lyons sandstone, the exterior walls are angled and separated so that stained-glass windows can be viewed from the exterior. A natural flow between the indoors and outdoors

(TOP) BOTH STONE AND STAINED GLASS ARE USED ON THE TEMPLE'S MODERN EXTERIOR. (BOTTOM) MODERN STAINED GLASS ADDS LIGHT TO THE INTERIOR OF THE TEMPLE.

occurs because of the use of windows and materials that complement the environment. Due to the building's clean lines and expert design, it has remained visually pleasing and functional over the years. In 1989, the population of the congregation had expanded sufficiently to warrant an addition. Carefully designed by the local architectural firm of Barker, Rinker, and Seacat, and under the watchful eye of Goodman, who was retained as an advisor, the addition matched the existing materials and structural style.

On the interior, modern stained glass adds light to the pentagonal-shaped sanctuary where the Holy Ark, created of Colorado Yule marble, holds the Torah. Wings built on the sides of the sanctuary hold overflow on holy days and during special events. In addition, this building houses a variety of religious art and artifacts, including a large menorah made of stained glass and the Ten Commandments carved in Hebrew on an oak valance. The eternal light hangs in the sanctuary, depicted as a bronze starburst. Five thousand feet of clerestory windows were executed in the "dalle de verre" style by famed glass artist Robert Pinart. In this style, glass panels are handset into a concrete matrix.

The interior ceiling is a beautiful example of modern design.

# 3  MONTVIEW BOULEVARD PRESBYTERIAN CHURCH
## 1980 DAHLIA STREET

Architectural Style: RICHARDSONIAN ROMANESQUE, GOTHIC REVIVAL
Built: 1910, 1918, 1928, AND 1958   Cost: $270,000
Architects: HARRY JAMES MANNING, FRANK W. FREWEN JR.,
BURNHAM F. HOYT, AND MERRILL H. HOYT

Designated as one of the most visible landmarks in the Park Hill neighborhood of Denver, Montview Boulevard Presbyterian Church is a true example of a congregation that grew, yet focused on retaining, their church's architectural integrity as they expanded. Throughout the many additions to this building, it has remained a beautiful example of how additions to a building can complement each other.

Built as an answer to the growth of its community of Presbyterians in the Park Hill area, Montview has played a distinctive role in the community since that time. The church first built on the site hosted lectures and speakers from the community and political arena and special events hosted by the congregation. This was replaced with a stone chapel built in 1910. An addition to the chapel was built in 1918. An educational wing was added in 1928, designed by Hoyt and Hoyt. Between 1947 and 1967, the church saw tremendous growth and another larger wing was added to the church in 1958.

Montview did much to combat racial ignorance and ease tensions in the community as race restrictions in the area were lifted. In 1963, church members were asked to sign a nondiscriminatory pledge when buying and selling real estate. At the height of tension, Montview started a racially integrated preschool. On January 26, 1964, Martin Luther King Jr. spoke at the church to a group of more than 3,000 people. Today the church hosts a variety of programming services for the community, including tutoring and mentorship for youth.

The original chapel building built in 1910 is constructed of rhyolite stone with a highly pitched cross-gable roof in a rectangular plan. The building has rounded arch openings and windows with stained glass created by Paul Helleck. The 1918 two-story addition was carefully

A RECESSED ENTRY PORTAL IS CAPPED BY DECORATIVE ELEMENTS.

designed by Manning and Frewen to integrate with and complement the chapel. Rhyolite stone is used extensively and the arched openings and roof of the addition mimic the chapel. In 1928, a Richardsonian Romanesque-style education wing designed by Burnham and Merrill Hoyt, was added in the form of an octagonal-shaped main room, with a wing attached and square and arched windows. Finally, in 1958, a two-story rectangular building built in Gothic Revival Style was added, which harmonizes well with the previous additions.

The interior of the church houses a mix of stained-glass windows, including historic as well as newer windows. The interior sanctuary is framed by the pipes from the original organ and is now used as a theater. Decorative plaster banding crosses the ceiling and surrounds the room. The newest portion of the church has a large sanctuary that is home to a collection of stained-glass windows and a pointed, arched vaulted ceiling.

THE DECORATIVE CUPOLA IS A TREASURE ON THE 1918 SECTION OF THE BUILDING.

A BEAUTIFUL ORGAN, HISTORIC LIGHTING, AND A GRAND VIEW OF THE ROSE WINDOW GRACE THE INTERIOR OF THE 1958 SANCTUARY.

# 4 PARK HILL UNITED METHODIST CHURCH
## 5209 MONTVIEW BOULEVARD

NR

Architectural Style: SPANISH COLONIAL REVIVAL
Built: 1924, 1956  Cost: $75,000
Architects: WILLIAM N. BOWMAN; 1956 ADDITION WALTER H. SIMON

Considered one of the best examples of Spanish Colonial Revival architecture in Denver, the 1924 Park Hill United Methodist Church has been a landmark in the Park Hill neighborhood since the mid-twenties.

By 1912, Park Hill was one of Denver's most fashionable districts. The site at Montview and Forest was chosen for a church to serve those moving to this burgeoning community. Over the decades, the congregation continued to grow, and in 1956 the church built a Romanesque addition to house its almost 2,500 members.

The original church was designed by William N. Bowman and is unique to his design repertoire. It is one of only four buildings that he executed in this style. The remaining three are located in Alamosa, Colorado.

The church was designed with an L-shaped plan in the Spanish Colonial Revival style. Defining traits include a highly pitched cross-gable roof capped with red tile, wide overhanging eaves, smooth stucco walls, dormers, and parapets. A mission-like bell tower overlooks the courtyard, which is surrounded by a stucco and wrought-iron wall that makes it an enclosed plaza. The windows are housed in arched or rectangular openings, and the tower entrance is decorated with carved stonework. The 1956 extension, designed by Walter H. Simon, was built to mimic the original elements of the 1924 church. Featuring its own bell tower, the addition also has decorative stonework and arched windows.

The church's interior sanctuary, which seats 1,000, is finished in Flemish oak and complemented by stained-glass windows. The original organ was moved from the first sanctuary when the addition was built and expanded. Built by M. P. Moller Company, the organ contains almost 1,400 pipes.

HIGHLY DETAILED STONEWORK ADDS INTEREST TO THE SIMPLE ARCHED ENTRY AND TERRA-COTTA ROOF.

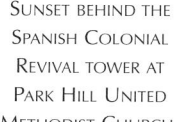

SUNSET BEHIND THE SPANISH COLONIAL REVIVAL TOWER AT PARK HILL UNITED METHODIST CHURCH.

# 5. ST. THOMAS EPISCOPAL CHURCH  DL
## 2201 DEXTER STREET

Architectural Style: SPANISH COLONIAL REVIVAL
Built: 1908–29   Cost: $55,500
Architect: HARRY JAMES MANNING

Hailed as the first designated Denver Landmark **DL** in 1977, St. Thomas Episcopal Church remains a key player in both the community and the architecture of the Park Hill neighborhood.

Saint Thomas–Park Hill Mission Church was started in 1908 at the request of Episcopal Bishop Charles Olmsted. Six Park Hill families met with the bishop and a committee was appointed to find a site. They were successful in locating four lots at the corner of 22nd and Dexter, and within twenty-four hours had the $6,000 in necessary funds to purchase the land. On September 6, 1916, the church's cornerstone was laid and the first building was completed.

After the mission became a parish in 1916, it grew rapidly and made plans to expand. In 1930, the building was completed that we know today as St. Thomas Episcopal Church.

Designed by Harry James Manning, the church is constructed in a Spanish Colonial Revival style. Elements of this style are evident in the exterior of the building, including the Churrigueresque entry, use of stucco and Spanish red tile roofing, and arched window and door openings. Special details include carved ecclesiastical symbols over the doors, an open courtyard contained in the U-shaped building, and an arcaded cloister.

The interior is in a cruciform plan and includes a nave, transept, side chancels, and arched chancel. Leaded-glass clerestory windows accent the sanctuary. The chancel holds such fine features as carved stone sedilias, oculus windows, and a handmade tile floor.

(TOP) LINING THE INTERIOR COURTYARD IS A COVERED WALKWAY WITH HISTORIC LIGHTS.
(BOTTOM) CARVED DETAILS ON THE DOUBLE ARCHES DECORATE THE INTERIOR AND ADD VISUAL APPEAL.

# EVANS MEMORIAL CHAPEL UNIVERSITY OF DENVER CAMPUS
2199 SOUTH VINE STREET

NR DL

Architectural Style: GOTHIC REVIVAL
Built: 1878  Cost: UNKNOWN  Architect: UNKNOWN

Erected by the famous Colorado Territorial Governor John Evans as a memorial to his daughter Josephine Evans Elbert, the Evans Memorial Chapel at the University of Denver is the oldest Protestant church building still in use in the city.

Before his term as the territorial governor, Evans was actively involved in politics, education, and business. Elected to the Electoral College, he was one of the first politicians to advocate for the emancipation of slaves and to allow their enlistment in the army in 1861 to crush the rebellion of the southern states. He played a major role in the development of Colorado from the beginning. In the early 1860s Evans realized the need for an institute for higher education in the region. After successfully advocating the establishment of Northwestern University in Evanston, Illinois, Evans set his sights on Denver.

After the establishment of the University of Denver, originally called Colorado Seminary, and at the request of Methodist church members, Evans built the church in honor of his daughter. The church was used on its original site as part of Grace Community Methodist Church. When threatened with demolition by the construction of a parking lot, it was moved stone by stone in 1959 to its present location on the University of Denver campus. All subsequent restoration and preservation efforts have been completed with extreme care to protect the integrity of the building.

The exterior of the chapel is simple in design, with heavily rusticated red sandstone articulated into a Gothic motif. Iron detailing highlights a steep pitched slate roof. Arched windows also accentuate the Gothic design.

The chapel's interior is simple in design as well. One large room comprises the structure in its entirety. The ceiling is characterized by open-tracery wood trusses, while pointed arched windows, which hold decorative geometric stained-glass panels, flank the nave.

(TOP) CAPPING THE SLATE SHINGLE ROOF FROM THIS SIDE VIEW IS DECORATIVE IRONWORK. (BOTTOM) HISTORIC LIGHTING FIXTURES AND DETAILED CEILING TRUSSES ARE PART OF THE SIMPLE INTERIOR.

# TOUR FOUR: SOUTHWEST DENVER

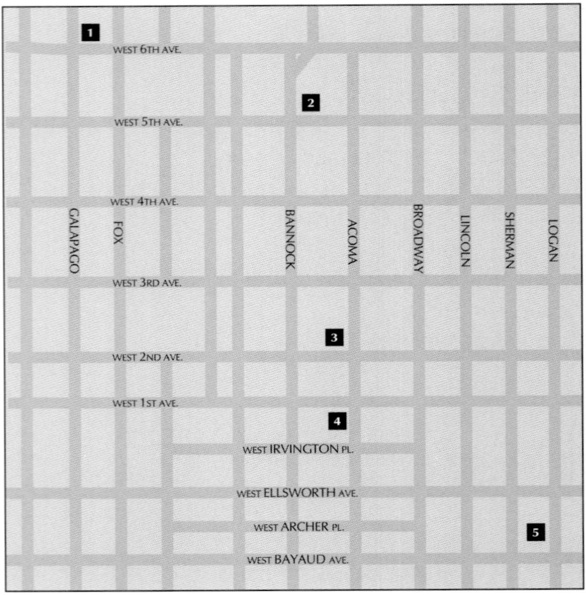

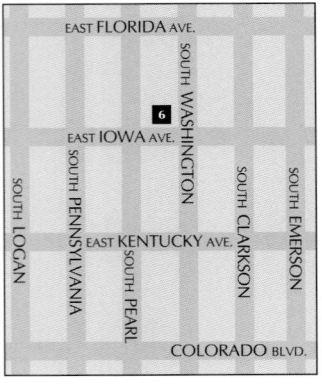

▲
North

# KEY

1. 600 Galapago Street
   (St. Joseph's Roman Catholic Church)
2. 201 West Fifth Avenue
   (Four Winds Survival Project)
3. 126 West Second Avenue
   (Episcopal Church of St. Peter and St. Mary)
4. 120 West First Avenue
   (First Avenue Presbyterian Church)
5. 216 South Grant Street
   (Grant Avenue United Methodist Church)
6. 1600 South Pearl Street
   (Cameron United Methodist Church)

# ST. JOSEPH'S ROMAN CATHOLIC CHURCH
## 600 GALAPAGO STREET

NR

Architectural Style: GOTHIC REVIVAL
Built: 1889  Cost: UNKNOWN  Architect: UNKNOWN

St. Joseph's reflects the changing history of Denver and the continuing need for carefully planned restoration and preservation. It was featured as an example of "Urban Sacred Places" which were listed as one of the eleven most endangered places in the United States in 2003 by the National Trust for Historic Preservation. The building's masonry and stonework, doors and windows have been meticulously restored, all in accordance with the Secretary of the Interior's Standards for Restoration and Preservation.

In 1889, St. Joseph's was the seventh Catholic church built in the city of Denver. Under the stewardship of the Redemptorist Fathers and Bishop Nicholas Matz, the church provided a spiritual and community cornerstone for a prosperous middle-class neighborhood comprised of German and Irish immigrants. The community changed significantly in 1922 when the majority of the residents in the neighborhood were laid off due to a decline in the railroad industry. Although membership declined as well, the parish remained intact and began to serve the working-class community of Denver that it still serves today. The neighborhood and parish community are now almost entirely Hispanic. The community's mix of low-income and migrant workers depends on the church for assistance, including access to a community food bank, counseling and emergency service referrals, and facilities for the homeless.

St. Joseph's Church is a modified two-story Gothic building that is irregular in plan. Located on the front facade of the building are two spires, which act as extensions of each side, and seven bays. Two separate smokestacks flank the rear of the building.

On the interior, exposed ceiling beams accent the sanctuary and provide a backdrop for the original historic hanging lamps. The church holds a collection of twelve Gothic stained-glass windows on both sides of the sanctuary, three triangular windows above the elaborate altar, and a large main window located on the front facade of the building.

(TOP) THE EXTERIOR OF ST. JOSEPH'S CHURCH IS TRIMMED IN WHITE WITH ELABORATE SPIRES THAT TOP TOWERS ON THE FRONT FACADE.
(BOTTOM) ABOVE THE ELABORATE ALTAR IS A GOTHIC WINDOW REPRESENTATIVE OF THE STYLE CLEARLY EVIDENT IN THE REMAINDER OF THE CHURCH.

# FOUR WINDS SURVIVAL PROJECT D&L
## 201 WEST FIFTH AVENUE

Architectural Style: GOTHIC REVIVAL
Built: 1912   Cost: UNKNOWN
Architects: HAROLD AND VIGGIO BAERRESEN

Called by some one of the most unique sacred places in Denver, the Four Winds Survival Project is working to preserve and maintain Native American cultures in a building originally created to house a Lutheran congregation. Initially called Danish Evangelical Bethany Lutheran Church, this site is an example of how a sacred place can be used creatively to meet the needs of a community.

Located in the Baker Historic District along with other ethnic churches, Four Winds was built by two brothers, Harold and Viggio Baerresen, shipbuilders from Denmark. Designed for a Danish congregation, services in Danish were held at the site until 1930. The Danish congregation remained until the 1980s. In 1989, the Four Winds Survival Project moved onto the site.

The vision of Four Winds is to maintain the traditions of Native Americans in a quiet corner of a busy metropolitan area. Traditional quilting and beadwork are taught so that members can reconnect with their heritage, and a wide variety of services are offered to members, including food, clothing, human services referrals, and job assistance programs.

Built as a two-story rectangular-shaped building with a steep cross-gabled roof, decorative finials, distinct segmented arches, and decorative brick crenellations, this building is considered an example of Gothic Revival–style architecture. A large, square steeple dominates the southeast corner of the building and provides a visual landmark for the neighborhood.

The interior of the building is simple in nature, with a domed wood ceiling, stained woodwork, and an altar behind a pointed arch in the north wall. Stained-glass windows of simple design add visual accents, and a large rose window towers over a raised choir loft.

Four Winds provides an example of Gothic architecture in a neighborhood setting.

Simple colored stained glass is a highlight of this inner-city sacred place.

# 3 EPISCOPAL CHURCH OF ST. PETER AND ST. MARY
## 126 WEST SECOND AVENUE

D&L

Architectural Style: ENGLISH COUNTRY/ECLECTIC
Built: 1891  Cost: UNKNOWN  Architects: C. H. LEE AND T. D. BOAL

Since its inception, the Episcopal Church of St. Peter and St. Mary has both prospered and struggled, serving the poor Cornish miners in Denver and working-class families who lived near the railroad lines. One parishioner has commented, "The history of St. Peter's Episcopal Church can be compared to the peaks and valleys of the Rocky Mountains."

Started by a small group of homesick Cornish miners and railroad workers who desired a church that could act as a social and spiritual center for the community, the group approached Bishop John Spalding for approval. The bishop was receptive to the idea and worked to secure land from a wealthy Denver widower. On November 29, 1891, Canon Charles H. Marshall of St. John's Cathedral laid the cornerstone. The parish was named the Mission Church of St. Peter after the home church of many of the congregants in Cornwall, England. Designed by C. H. Lee and T. D. Boal, the parish house was completed first, and meetings were held at that site until the building could be completed.

With the unfolding of the Silver Panic of 1893, the completion of the church was stalled due to financial reasons and the rector resigned. Services continued to be held at the parish house, and in 1916 the congregation built a foundation for a parish hall. They roofed it and used it as the site of the parish hall for more than thirty years. Today the church serves the local community through a weekly Tuesday night St. Clare Supper and serving "Meals on Wheels" through the Volunteers of America. The sewing guild provides over 250 garments yearly to the Denver branch of the Needlework Guild of America.

Through good times and bad, the church has survived because of the ingenuity of its members. The church is topped with a cross that was originally from a house at 1154 Broadway, where St. Mark's had its earliest beginnings. When the church moved, the new owner took down

THE BEAUTY OF THE EXTERIOR OF THIS ENGLISH-STYLE CHURCH IS EVIDENT.

the cross and disposed of it. A member of St. Peter's found it and brought it home to his church. The cross remains today. In the early beginnings of the church, members would collect coal near the railroad tracks that had fallen off the coal tenders from passing locomotives and would then carefully bring it back to the church to warm the parishioners on Sunday mornings. When families could not support a salary for the rector, they gave in-kind food donations instead.

The exterior of the church was constructed in an English style and has a steep roof with deep overhangs, large wood brackets, and hip roof bays. A rectangular tower stands over the central recessed arched entrance, which is protected by iron grills. The exterior is comprised of rusticated Castle Rock rhyolite stone and wood trim.

The interior of the church has remained a testament to the courage and determination of its congregation. A wrought-iron fence encloses the sanctuary, which houses wood pews, an organ, and decorative stained-glass windows. Hal Kendig, who was the longest-standing member of the church, donated the Apostles window and the door between the vestibule and the church interior.

(TOP) IVY DECORATES THE PORCH ON THE EXTERIOR. (LEFT) ITS SOLID WOOD CEILING ADDS TO THE RICHNESS OF THE SANCTUARY.

# 4  FIRST AVENUE PRESBYTERIAN CHURCH
## 120 WEST FIRST AVENUE

Architectural Style: GOTHIC REVIVAL
Built: 1891, 1906  Cost: UNKNOWN  Architect: MONTANA FALLIS

Known as a key landmark of the Baker Historical District, First Avenue Presbyterian Church has played a vital role in the diverse community of South Denver through programming, historic restoration and preservation, and as a host site for a variety of community activities.

Started in 1889 as The Church of the Redeemer, the first congregation built a small red brick octagonal chapel in 1891. The chapel still stands today. A later merger with Capitol Avenue Church and Denver's First Presbyterian Church created the current congregation of First Avenue Presbyterian. The current building, constructed of buff brick, which blends well with the surrounding Baker Landmark Historic District, now surrounds the original chapel.

Historically, the neighborhood was home to a diverse group of residents of European heritage, including German, Irish, Scottish, and English. The district was the home of mountain man Jim Beckwourth and early pioneers William and Elizabeth Byers. Cable cars from the Broadway district gave the working class residents who resided here easy access to work in the city or at the smelters.

Designed by Montana Fallis, the 1906 building embodies characteristics of a Gothic Revival structure through its steeply pitched roof and tall steeple. Additionally, the building has detailed pointed arches, which add to the exterior design of the structure.

Reflecting the Gothic style of the exterior, the interior hosts a variety of architectural features: these include stained glass in windows and doors, an intricately carved wood altar, and religious artwork.

(TOP) VISITORS TO THIS IMPORTANT LANDMARK ARE WELCOMED BY THE GOTHIC DOORS ON THE EXTERIOR. (BOTTOM) DETAILING ON THE WOOD ALTAR SHOWS THE CARE PUT INTO THE CREATION OF THE FURNISHINGS OF THIS CHURCH.

# GRANT AVENUE UNITED METHODIST CHURCH
## 216 SOUTH GRANT STREET

Architectural Style: GOTHIC REVIVAL
Built: 1908  Cost: UNKNOWN  Architect: HARRY JAMES MANNING

As the first Methodist church on the south side of Denver, Grant Avenue United Methodist Church exemplifies how the placement of a parish can directly affect the community it serves.

After outgrowing meetings in a tent church, then parsonage and chapel, the congregation purchased the site adjacent to the structure and constructed a sanctuary and auditorium, designed by architect Harry Manning, which were carefully attached to the parsonage and chapel. In 1920, an addition was built to make room for a new community building, also designed by Manning.

The congregation has played a major role in the church's community programming. The War Work Enterprise program, started in 1918, trained pastors for chaplainship in the military. In 1937, the congregation started the Youth Roundup program, providing activities to keep youth out of mischief. After World War II, the church established the School for Christian Living, which promoted religious and social tolerance. Today the site is used as a community center, and houses several congregations and community groups.

Several prominent Coloradans have been associated with this parish, including Margaret E. Scheve, the first woman Methodist minister in Colorado, and Rev. Laird V. Loveland, a famous international missionary.

Manning, considered to be one of Denver's finest architects, blended style and materials in the construction of this church. The building is accentuated with a steeple, typical of the Gothic style, which is capped by a terra-cotta roof. Decorative brickwork enhances the various facades.

The mix of the Gothic Revival and Arts and Craft styles is evident in the interior, with its impressive trusses and woodwork. Arched windows accent the decorative features and make a welcoming sanctuary.

(TOP) IMPRESSIVE TRUSSES ACCENT THE INTERIOR SPACES OF THE BUILDING. (BOTTOM) THE TERRA-COTTA ROOF ACCENTS THE BUILDING, WHICH HAS DECORATIVE BRICKWORK ON ITS TALL STEEPLE.

# CAMERON UNITED METHODIST CHURCH
1600 SOUTH PEARL STREET

D&L

Architectural Style: GOTHIC REVIVAL AND ROMANESQUE
Built: 1909–13  Cost: UNKNOWN  Architect: THOMAS T. BARBER

Cameron United Methodist Church has played an integral role in the history of its south Denver neighborhood, Platte Park. Originally established as Fleming's Grove Methodist Church, the oldest Methodist congregation in south Denver, the church still serves the community in a variety of ways.

To house a growing congregation, the present building was commissioned in 1909 after a donation was received from the Cameron family through the Methodist Church Extension Society.

Through both religious and secular programming, the church has long been a center for the community. From the church's inception, the congregation has hosted community recitals and concerts and projects that serve the needs of the poor. Today the congregation continues this commitment by providing a venue for community forums, artistic and cultural presentations, and gatherings that focus on political and economic issues relevant to the neighborhood. Cameron is the "community center" of the Platte Park Neighborhood.

Renowned architect Thomas Barber designed the building in an eclectic style, using Romanesque elements such as smooth-faced walls and rounded arches. Characteristics of the Gothic Revival style can also be seen in the steep pitch of the gabled roofs and the unique towers. The building remains virtually unaltered from its original state.

Within the Classical Revival sanctuary is a collection of four large stained-glass windows, created and installed by artist Frank Watkins after an apprenticeship under his father, Clarence Watkins.

The Watkins Stained Glass Studio remains a center of meticulous artistic work in both new and preserved glass and is testament to the vision of a family of artists who have maintained it in the Denver area for more than one hundred years. Today, Phil Watkins Jr. continues to create and restore outstanding examples of stained glass in the region.

(TOP) THE DOME OF THE CEILING CROWNS OVER THE GOTHIC CHURCH WITH INTRICATE CRENELLATIONS IN THE TOWER. (BOTTOM) WOOD MOLDINGS AND PLASTER DETAILS ON THE INTERIOR ARE FURTHER EVIDENCE OF CLASSICAL DETAILING.

# TOUR FIVE: CENTRAL DENVER

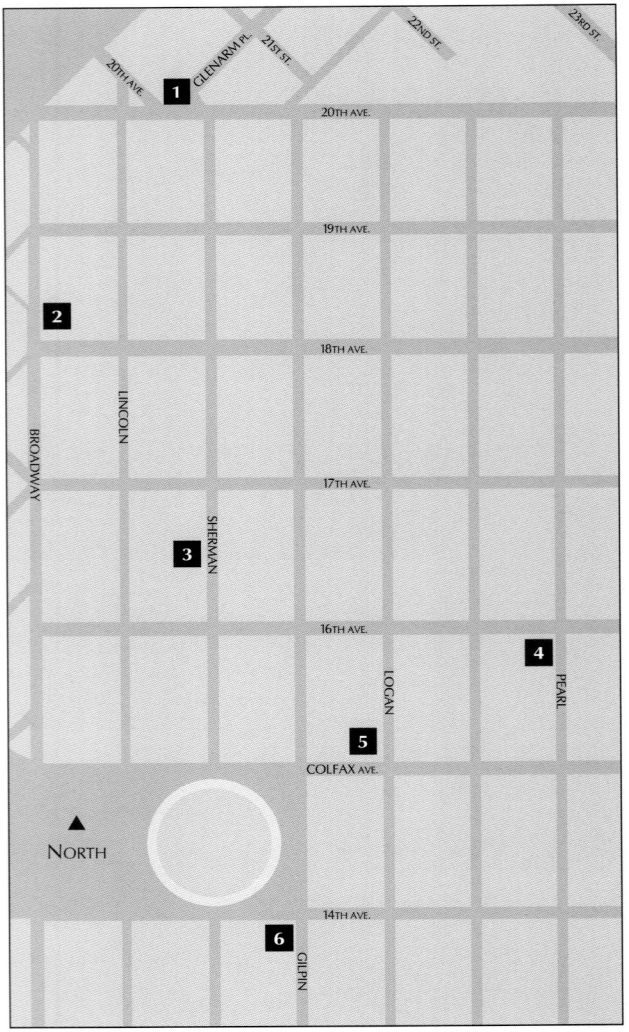

# KEY

1. 2015 Glenarm Place
   (St. Andrew's Episcopal Church)
2. 1820 Broadway
   (Trinity United Methodist Church)
3. 1660 Sherman Street
   (Central Presbyterian Church)
4. 1595 Pearl Street
   (Temple Events Center)
5. 1530 Logan Street
   (Cathedral of the Immaculate Conception)
6. 1345 Grant Street
   (First Baptist Church)

# ST. ANDREW'S EPISCOPAL CHURCH
## 2015 GLENARM PLACE

NR DL

Architectural Style: GOTHIC REVIVAL
Built: 1907   Cost: $45,000
Architects: RALPH ADAMS CRAM, JULES JACQUES BENOIS BENEDICT

St. Andrew's Episcopal Church, first known as Trinity Memorial Church, was founded in 1873. Erected in 1874 at 26th and Curtis, the church was established as the second Episcopal church in Denver. After the original church blew down in 1904, A. D. Parker of the Colorado and Southern Railway made a large donation of $11,500 and the church was built at its present location. Consecrated in 1907 and dedicated January 17, 1909, the church was half the size of the original.

The church was established in an upper-class neighborhood that soon transitioned to one of reduced circumstances due to the changing diversity of the neighborhood. The name was changed to St. Andrew's and its status became that of a mission church. In 1919 Rev. Neil Stanley, priest from 1928 to 1942, helped support the church by selling fiction stories to pulp magazines under a pseudonym. Father Stanley was also successful at bringing converts into the church. These converts were often generous in their contributions.

In 1969, the rector of St. Andrew's, Rev. John Marr Stark, formed the Order of the Holy Family. In 1970, the homeless were welcomed and given a place to sleep in the undercroft. Reverend Stark opened the church to runaway young people and served meals to those in need, the first pastor in Denver to do so. Other churches soon followed suit. In 1974, St. Andrew's became the site of a Canonically Instituted Monastic Order and the only male-female order in the country. By 1986, the Order had moved to Santa Fe and the church was in a state of serious deterioration. It was again made a mission of St. John's Cathedral and the building was stabilized and restored to its former beauty.

Designed by famous American architect Ralph Adams Cram in 1903, this Gothic Revival church is built in an L-shape and is made of reddish-brown brick with sandstone trim. The roof is Vermont slate.

A carved statue sits on the exterior of the church.

This church is the only Colorado work of Cram and resembles his much larger work in Middletown, Rhode Island, St. George's Chapel. The parish house was designed by another famous architect, Jules Jacques Benois Benedict, and complements the main building without detracting from its original design.

The interior of this church is beautifully detailed with Gothic tracery and exposed wood beams. The church also houses a collection of leaded-glass windows, diamond-paned, with a modest quatrefoil ornamentation at the front window

(TOP) IN THIS ALCOVE, ORGAN PIPES AND HISTORICAL LIGHTING FEATURES FRAME THE LEADED-GLASS WINDOW. (BOTTOM) DECORATIVE FRAMES AND DETAILED STONEWORK GIVE THIS CHURCH A MEDIEVAL FEEL.

# TRINITY UNITED METHODIST CHURCH
## 1820 BROADWAY

Architectural Style: GOTHIC REVIVAL
Built: 1887–8  Cost: UNKNOWN  Architect: ROBERT S. ROESCHLAUB

Built by one of the oldest congregations in Denver, Trinity United Methodist Church is one of the most distinctive churches in what is now the central business district of downtown Denver. Still an active church today, it is a testament to the will and determination of a congregation working to preserve one of Denver's earliest churches.

The congregation first organized in 1859, the same year that Denver was founded. The most famous pastor of Trinity was Rev. Henry Buchtel, who later served as Colorado's governor from 1907 to 1909. Built in 1887–8, the building is an excellent example of Neo-Gothic architecture.

Designed by Robert S. Roeschlaub and located across from the Brown Palace Hotel, Trinity stands out as a representative of Denver's end of century building boom and as Roeschlaub's first and arguably greatest work in Denver. He conceived the church not as a whole plan but as a mix of many detailed and intricate elements. Roeschlaub hand drew every piece of the interior from the pews to the carving around the organ. The plans still exist today

Pointed gables and a tall dramatic stone tower steeple adorn the building's exterior. Built of rhyolite, a native volcanic stone from Castle Rock, Colorado, the building is light beige with hints of red and blue. The tower needs no supports because of the light weight of this type of stone. The church plan is derived from and is similar to Henry Hobson Richardson's Trinity Church in Boston.

On the interior, the stairways and three identical entrance portals lead to the grand entrance into the church's sanctuary. The majority of the stained glass that highlights the interior was designed by Healy and Millet of Chicago. Sixty-six lights hang above the pipe organ in honor of the books of the Bible. The organ, built in 1888 at a cost of $30,000 by Hilbourne Roosevelt, a cousin of Theodore, is the largest American-built organ of the nineteenth century still in operation.

(TOP) A TRIPLE-ARCHED RECESSED ENTRY. (BOTTOM) HERE A FACE CARVED IN STONE OVERLOOKS THE WINDOWS.

## 3. CENTRAL PRESBYTERIAN CHURCH  NR
### 1660 SHERMAN STREET

Architectural Style: ROMANESQUE REVIVAL
Built: 1891–2   Cost: MAIN BUILDING, $165,000; ADDITION, $500,000
Architect: FRANK E. EDBROOKE

Established as an outgrowth of the First Presbyterian Church of Denver, Central Presbyterian was named in 1874, reflecting a division between new- and old-school factions in the church. The board of trustees of the church included prominent members of the Denver community, such as William Larimer, George. W. Clayton, and Capt. Richard Sopris, a founder and mayor of Denver.

Designed during a period of important early growth in Denver, the red sandstone building represents some of the best work of architect Frank E. Edbrooke. Considered to be one of the major architects in nineteenth-century Denver, Edbrooke was responsible for the development of this large square church, which has crossing gables of equal height and length. Described by Richard Brettell in his book *Historic Denver* as "spare, simple, and colorstically unified," the church is accentuated by a tall thin tower with lantern openings, topped by ogee arches. In 1957, a wing for youth and education programs was added to the building and was carefully integrated into the overall design of the church

The building is designed in a crucifix shape. The apse end of the church is used as the entrance to the sanctuary, where the rose window has become the backdrop for the altar, pulpit, and choir loft. At the request of the original congregation, the sanctuary slopes down to the pulpit, and boxes were installed on the main floor under the balconies, giving the sanctuary a theaterlike quality reminiscent of the Old Broadway Theatre, where the congregation met while the church was under construction. Some of the interior's special features include false fireplaces in the sanctuary, painted faux organ pipes that surround the actual pipes, and carved leaf-design woodwork popular during the period in which this church was built.

THE BEAUTY OF THE EXTERIOR OF THIS ENGLISH-STYLE CHURCH IS EVIDENT IN THIS PHOTO.

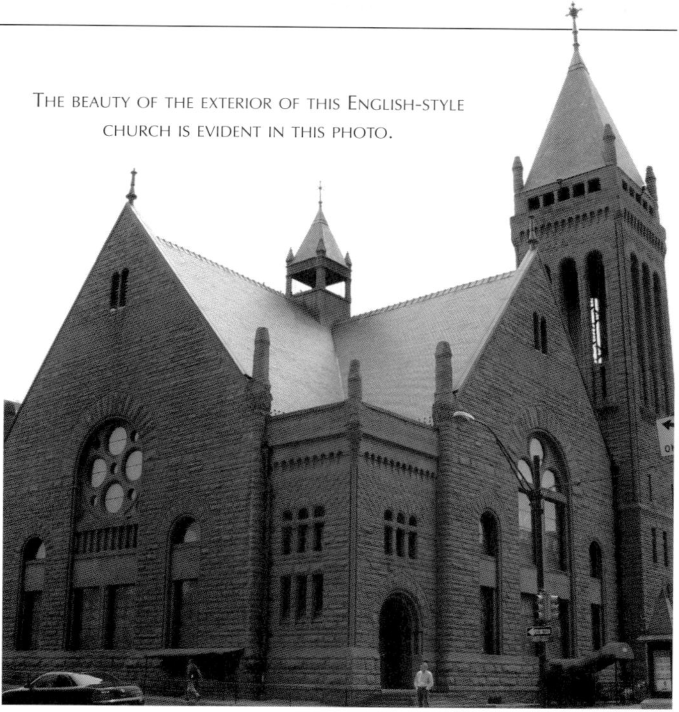

ITS SOLID WOOD CEILING AND ARCHES ADD TO THE RICHNESS OF THE SANCTUARY.

# TEMPLE EVENTS CENTER
## 1595 PEARL STREET

NR DL

Architectural Style: EXOTIC REVIVAL
Built: 1898, 1924  Cost: $37,000
Architects: JOHN J. HUMPHREYS, THIELMAN ROBERT WIEGER

Past home to Congregation Emanuel, the oldest Jewish congregation in the city, the Temple Events Center is an excellent example of a property used for a variety of purposes throughout its history. Saved from demolition by the city of Denver, and now supported by a private foundation, this site is now used as an event center for the wider community of Denver.

Constructed originally for Congregation Emanuel in 1898, the structure was the third temple built for a congregation that was growing fast and that had just lost its second temple home due to fire. Designed by John J. Humphreys in a Moorish style, the temple was dedicated in 1899 by Denver Mayor Thomas McMurray, Colorado Governor Charles Thomas, and ministers of seven different religious congregations. The festivities continued for three days and were attended by some of the largest crowds in the history of Denver. It is one of only three surviving Moorish-influenced synagogues in the country and is recognized as an outstanding example of a preserved sacred place that is being actively used by a community.

By 1908, the congregation was growing substantially and made plans to build a new temple at the site of the Capitol Hill cemetery. Because of the high cost, the idea was scrapped, and an addition was built adjacent to the structure. The addition was designed by Thielman Robert Wieger and built in 1924.

In 1956, the property was sold to the First Southern Baptist Church, and the last Jewish services were held in May of 1957. First Southern Baptist Church used the site until it was sold to Lovingway Church. In 1982, the property was sold to a private developer. Threatened with demolition in 1986, it was purchased by the City and County of Denver. The city then sold it to the Pearl Street Temple Emanuel Foundation. In 1988, the foundation "assumed the responsibility to restore the building and make it

Moorish influence is reflected in the exterior details of the tower and church.

available for use to the community." As this guide was going to print, a contract was in place for the sale of the Temple Events Center to the Colorado Ballet for their offices, ballet school and a presentation space.

The Temple Events Center is a multistory masonry structure. The original 1898 structure is clad in buff brick veneer, and the east facade is symmetrical in design. Octagonal towers with Moorish-style belvederes at their tops are located near the corners of this facade and host a projecting walkway around the top with a decorative railing. Detailed dentil molding crowns the top of the walls and adds interest to the main entry, which is highlighted by a set of Moorish-style entry doors. Exterior details include a variety of stained-glass windows and carved stonework details that reflect the original congregation by displaying multiple uses of the Star of David motif.

The most significant interior space is the auditorium, which is paneled in dark oak and which has a double-vaulted ceiling with decorative painting. The lower level holds a ballroom, which is part of the 1924 addition, and a library that was originally a rabbi's study. It features dark stained built-in book display cases and paneled ceilings and is one of the most treasured rooms at this site.

DECORATIVE CEILING TILES ACCENT THE INTERIOR.

STONEWORK SHOWS THE STAR OF DAVID DETAILING, REFLECTIVE OF THE ORIGINAL CONGREGATION.

# CATHEDRAL OF THE IMMACULATE CONCEPTION
## 1530 LOGAN STREET

NR DL

Architectural Style: GOTHIC REVIVAL
Built: 1902–12  Cost: $500,000
Architects: LEON COQUARD, AARON M. GOVE AND THOMAS F. WALSH

Located in the Civic Center historic district, the spires of the Cathedral of the Immaculate Conception complement the gold dome of the State Capitol. The congregation of St. Mary's, the predecessor to the cathedral in the small mining camp of Denver, included some of the area's most prominent citizens, such as John K. Mullen, John F. Campion, and Mrs. J. J. Brown (later memorialized as "Unsinkable Molly"). This congregation was determined to build a cathedral to the dogma of the Immaculate Conception of St. Mary and worked under the Rev. Hugh L. McMenamin and Bishop Nicholas Matz to raise the funds necessary to build what many called the "Pinnacled Glory of the West."

Ground was broken in 1902. Due to the substantial cost, construction was delayed. On October 27, 1912, His Eminence John Cardinal Farley of New York dedicated the cathedral. Thousands gathered for the elaborate ceremony, which officially designated this building as one of the grandest Catholic churches in the West and an example of the skills and aspirations of a pioneer community.

Constructed of dressed Indiana Bedford limestone on a foundation of Gunnison granite, the cathedral is an example of Gothic Revival style. The design by Leon Coquard, which was later realized by Aaron M. Gove and Thomas F. Walsh, was greatly influenced by the French cathedral at Amiens. Architectural elements include the vaulted ceilings, flying buttress, pinnacles, and clerestory. The structure represents excellence in local engineering and the ventilation system is a unique example of early air-conditioning. Constructed by men from the mining industry of Denver, this building reflects their knowledge and ingenuity.

Interior highlights include a main and side altars of Carrara marble, exquisite German stained glass, statuary, and spiral staircases leading to balconies that give a 180-mile view of the Rocky Mountain Range.

The decorative metal entry doors with the shield of the Archbishop add visual texture to the exterior.

The exterior is a dramatic addition to the cityscape along Colfax Avenue.

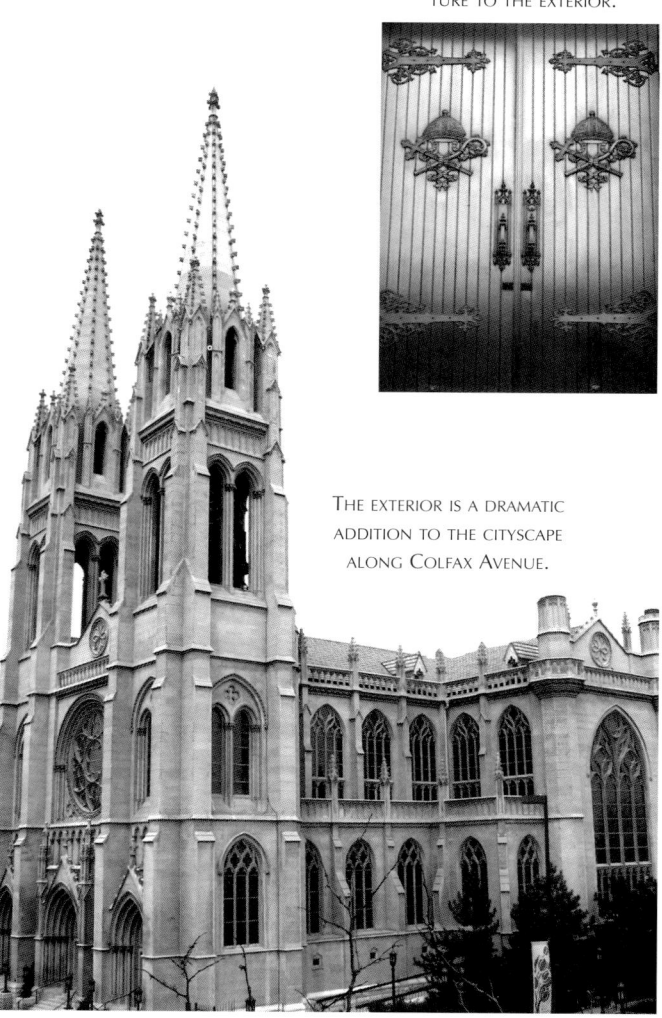

# FIRST BAPTIST CHURCH
## 1345 GRANT STREET

Architectural Style: CLASSICAL REVIVAL
Built: 1938  Cost: $253,711  Architect: GEORGE MEREDITH MUSICK SR.

Founded by Rev. Walter McDuffie Potter in 1864, the congregation of First Baptist Church was housed in three different locations until it found a permanent home across from the State Capitol building.

In July of 1919, the church purchased land from the Tritch estate. Because of the unsettled conditions after World War I and the Depression that followed in the thirties, the church was hesitant to begin construction and waited until 1934 to hire an architect and begin the project. With the leadership of Dr. Clarence Kemper, a pastor known for his commitment and success in building churches, the church was completed in 1938.

Designed by George Meredith Musick Sr., the building was constructed in true Georgian style and mimicked the design of many other Baptist churches in the United States. The building is built in the shape of a T, with outstanding architectural features, including the massive granite columns at the north entrance and the spire and weather vane, which have become landmarks in the downtown area.

The interior reflects the Georgian influence as well, with decorative moldings, draperies, and a vaulted ceiling. By 1950, a 126 rank Aolian-Skinner grand pipe organ was installed in the sanctuary.

(LEFT) THE INTERIOR FRONT PULPIT IS A PRIME EXAMPLE OF A DIVIDED PEDIMENT IN GEORGIAN STYLE. (BOTTOM) THE INFLUENCE OF GEORGIAN ARCHITECTURE IS AN INTEGRAL PART OF THIS CHURCH AND IS REFLECTED IN THIS VIEW OF THE STEEPLE.

# Sources

*In addition to the books and Web sites that follow, the author relied heavily on documentation found in the collections of the Colorado Historical Society, the COMPASS System, and the Sacred Landmarks Preservation Project, as well as on information from the Denver Landmark Preservation Commission and the archives of individual churches profiled in this guide*

Brettell, Richard R. *Historic Denver: The Architects and Architecture, 1858–1893.* Denver: Historic Denver, Inc., 1973.

Bucher, Ward. *Dictionary of Building Preservation.* Washington, DC: Wiley & Sons, 1996.

Episcopal Church of St. Peter and St. Mary, 100th Anniversary Booklet, 1991.

Fielder, John, and William Henry Jackson. *Colorado 1870–2000.* Denver: Westcliffe Publishers, 1999.

Gibson, Barbara. *The Lower Downtown Historic District.* Denver: Denver Museum of Nature and Science and Historic Denver, Inc., 1995.

Noel, Thomas J. *Denver Landmarks and Historic Districts.* Niwot: University Press of Colorado, 1996.

———. *Colorado Catholicism and the Archdiocese of Denver, 1857–1989.* Niwot: University Press of Colorado, 1989.

———, and Barbara S. Norgren. *Denver: The City Beautiful and Its Architects.* Denver: Historic Denver, Inc., 1987 (1993 Reprint).

SUGGESTED WEB SITES

Historic Denver, Inc./Sacred Landmarks Preservation Program
www.historicdenver.org
Information about Historic Denver's programs, including the grassroots program in Denver working to restore and preserve historic sacred places.

Colorado Historical Society
www.coloradohistory.org
The home page of the Colorado Historical Society that will link you to the various departments and services providing Colorado history information.

National Trust for Historic Preservation
www.nationaltrust.org
The premier national organization working to preserve historic landmarks in the United States and its territories.

Partners for Sacred Places
www.sacredplaces.org
A national program working to restore and preserve sacred places.

# Church Index

Annunciation Catholic Church, 14
Asbury Methodist Episcopal Church, 34

Cameron United Methodist Church, 72
Cathedral of the Immaculate Conception, 88
Central Presbyterian Church, 82
Chapel of Our Merciful Savior, 28

Denver Gospel Church, 16

Episcopal Church of St. Peter and St. Mary, 64
Evans Memorial Chapel, 56

First Avenue Presbyterian Church, 68
First Baptist Church, 90
First Divine Science Church of Denver, 42
Four Winds Survival Project, 62

Grant Avenue United Methodist Church, 70

Holy Transfiguration of Christ Cathedral, 10

Montview Boulevard Presbyterian Church, 48

Our Lady of Mount Carmel Church, 52

Park Hill United Methodist Church, 38

Sacred Heart Catholic Church, 12
St. Andrew's Episcopal Church, 76
St. Dominic's Church, 32
St. Ignatius Loyola Church, 18
St. Joseph's Roman Catholic Church, 60
St. Patrick's Church, 36
St. Paul's United Methodist Church, 20
St. Thomas Episcopal Church, 54

Temple Emanuel, 44
Temple Events Center, 84
Trinity United Methodist Church, 80

Zen Center of Denver, 30
Zion Baptist Church, 22

# BIOGRAPHICAL INDEX

Asbury, Francis, 34
Ascell, Rev. Dr. Robert, 16

Baerresen, Harold, 62
Baerresen, Viggio, 62
Barber, Thomas T., 72
Beckwourth, Jim, 68
Benedict, Jacques, 42, 76, 78
Boal, T. D., 64
Bowman, William N., 52
Brooks, Nona L., 42
Brown, Mrs. J. J. ("Unsinkable Molly"), 88
Buchtel, Rev. Henry, 80
Byers, Elizabeth, 68
Byers, William, 68

Cabrini, Frances, 38
Campion, John F., 88
Carrigan, Fr. Joseph, 36
Clark, Ira, 22
Clayton, George W., 82
Cram, Ralph Adams, 76

Damascio, Frank, 38

Edbrooke, Frank E., 82
Eddy, Rev. Mary Baker, 30
Elbert, Josephine Evans, 56
Evans, Colorado Terr. Gov. John, 56

Fallis, Montana, 68
Farley, John Cardinal, 88
Felton, Rufus K., 24
Ford, Rev. John E., 22
Ford, Justina Warren, 22
Frewen, Frank W. Jr., 18, 48

Goodman, Percival, 44, 46
Gove, Aaron M., 88
Greeley, Julia, 12
Guadalupe, Our Lady of, 12

Helleck, Paul, 48
Hoyt, Burnham F., 30, 48, 50
Hoyt, Merrill H., 30, 48, 50
Humphreys, John J., 34, 84

Jackson, Frank H., 22
Jackson, Jesse, 22
Johnson, James Weldon, 24

Kemper, Dr. Clarence, 90
Kendig, Hal, 66
King, Martin Luther Jr., 48

Lamm, Richard, 24
Larimer, William, 82
Lee, C. H., 64
Lepore, Fr. Mariano, 38
Liggins, Rev. William Theodore, 22
Loveland, Rev. Laird V., 70

Machebeuf, Bishop Joseph, 36
Manning, Harry James, 36, 48, 54, 70
Marshall, Canon Charles H., 64
Matz, Bishop Nicholas, 32, 36, 38, 60
McDonnell, Fr. Charles, 18
McGlynn, Fr. Tom, 32
McMenamin, Rev. Hugh, 88
Meyer, Franz, 14
Mountjoy, Frank E., 18
Mullen, John K., 88
Murdoch, James, 28
Murphy, Fr. J. T., 32
Musick, George Meredith Sr., 90

Norrid, William, 22

Olmsted, Bishop Charles, 54

Parker, A. D., 76
Pinart, Robert, 46
Potter, Rev. Walter McDuffie, 22, 90

Randolph, A. Phillip, 24
Richardson, Henry Hobson, 80
Rivinius, George F., 22
Robinson, Fr. Henry, 14
Roeschlaub, Robert S., 80

Scheve, Margaret E., 70
Schroeder, Pat, 24
Schwaezler, Anton, 18
Simon, Walter H., 52
Sopris, Capt. Richard, 82
Spalding, Bishop John, 64
Speer, Mayor Robert, 30
Stanley, Rev. Neil, 76
Stark, Rev. John Marr, 76
Strong, Walter, 24

Tabor, Elizabeth "Baby Doe," 12
Tabor, Horace, 12

Wagner, F. C., 36
Walsh, Thomas F., 88
Watkins, Clarence, 72
Watkins, Frank, 72
Watkins, Phil Jr., 72
Webb, Mayor Wellington, 24
Webb, Rep. Wilma G., 24
Wesley, John, 34
Wieger, Thielman Robert, 84
Willison, Robert, 32
Wright, Frank Lloyd, 44

Zeniuk, Nickolai, 10
Zettler, F. X., 14

A SIMPLE SILHOUETTE OF THE BELL TOWER OF ST. THOMAS EPISCOPAL CHURCH (PAGE 54) IS A LANDMARK IN THE PARK HILL NEIGHBORHOOD.

# NOTES